A CURSED
BLESSING

MY EMPATHIC JOURNEY

Victoria Kay
& Kasey Hannah

BALBOA.
PRESS
A DIVISION OF HAY HOUSE

Balboa Press books may be ordered through booksellers or by contacting:

Balboa Press
A Division of Hay House
1663 Liberty Drive
Bloomington, IN 47403
www.balboapress.com
1 (877) 407-4847

Because of the dynamic nature of the Internet, any web addresses or
links contained in this book may have changed since publication and
may no longer be valid. The views expressed in this work are solely those
of the author and do not necessarily reflect the views of the publisher,
and the publisher hereby disclaims any responsibility for them.

The author of this book does not dispense medical advice or prescribe the use
of any technique as a form of treatment for physical, emotional, or medical
problems without the advice of a physician, either directly or indirectly. The
intent of the author is only to offer information of a general nature to help
you in your quest for emotional and spiritual well-being. In the event you use
any of the information in this book for yourself, which is your constitutional
right, the author and the publisher assume no responsibility for your actions.

Any people depicted in stock imagery provided by Thinkstock are models,
and such images are being used for illustrative purposes only.
Certain stock imagery © Thinkstock.

Print information available on the last page.

ISBN: 978-1-5043-4722-8 (sc)
ISBN: 978-1-5043-4724-2 (hc)
ISBN: 978-1-5043-4723-5 (e)

Library of Congress Control Number: 2015920472

Balboa Press rev. date: 01/07/2016

CONTENTS

Acknowledgements ix

Introduction.. xi

Foreword xiii

Prologue xv

PART ONE MY CURSE

Chapter 1   My Early Years 3

Chapter 2   The "Curse" Begins 12

Chapter 3   Almost Pregnant 20

Chapter 4   Just Hormones...25

Chapter 5   Nine Months and Counting........................29

Chapter 6   Going Into Business...................................34

Chapter 7   Third and Final 46

PART TWO MY BLESSING

Chapter 8   Delivering Heaven's Message 61

Chapter 9   Meeting Jan..65

Chapter 10   First Spirit Visitation................................69

Chapter 11   A Message for Dominic 72

Chapter 12   What WILL My Family Think? 76

Chapter 13   And the Beat Goes On 79

Chapter 14   My Church 86

Afterword...89

Afterward...91

A CURSED BLESSING

This is the story of one woman's journey as an Empath, who realized that her depression, anxiety and physical illness did not, in fact, belong to her. Through spiritual guidance and research, she has discovered her amazing ability to communicate with the spirit world, and more.

Victoria Kay
With Kasey Hannah

Acknowledgements

I would like to acknowledge the tremendous support from my family and friends. Because of their love and understanding, I am now able to live my soul's purpose by bringing peace and healing to others.

I would like to give special acknowledgment and thanks to my best friend, Kasey, for her help in writing this book. I would also like to thank my father for his help with the editing. If not for these two people, I would not have the words to reach the people who I think will benefit most from reading this book.

INTRODUCTION

In life we may feel that we are less than our fellow man. Maybe we are not "as pretty as her", or "as smart as him", or maybe we feel that we are a "little inferior to others", or "a little damaged" in some way. We tend to accept this, without even thinking that maybe, just maybe, there is something different and special about us. We begin to accept and believe that we have great limitations, and we live our lives accordingly.

This is how I led my life until I could no longer accept this in my heart. My soul had a purpose, and this purpose needed to emerge. This book is about the battle for my life and the discovery of my abilities. I was blessed by God's grace to be able to emerge from the other side, with the ability to heal. I may never have known about these gifts, if I had not been blessed with my struggles, pain, and heartache. I want to share my story so that you may know that we all can emerge bigger and brighter than we ever could have imagined. I have learned that we only need to ask God for his strength, and to have faith that it will be delivered.

Blessed are you, who have mountains to climb, for you have been given the opportunity to embrace higher conscientiousness.

FOREWORD
Dr. Stacey Maxwell

At some point in our school of life, we face darkness, which may show up differently for each one of us. Yet, it all originates from our fear of not being enough on some level; emotionally, mentally, physically or spiritually. In this book, Victoria shares her life's experience of owning her personal power, standing in her light of magnificence, and discovering her purpose at a Soul level.

Not always will our spiritual guidance make sense to others, or at times, even to ourselves. It is when we listen within, and when we are willing to take the courageous steps from our heart's and soul's promptings, regardless of what we may see around us, and solely trusting in the Divine, that we become a witness to the blessings and miracles of life, and to becoming our fullest essence of Being. You are so much bigger and more significant than anyone has ever told you.

Victoria intimately shares with you her struggles to overcome the darkness of what she felt might possibly diminish her light, and instead, how it actually brought her through, bigger, stronger and better than ever before. Discovering her purpose and her innate magnificence, Victoria now shines her light so brightly that it illuminates a pathway for others to find their way out of the darkness!

For those who are seeking, you will see many parallels to mirror your own cherished life, regardless of what your "diagnosis" was or is. And it will empower you to become the fullest expression of self that you were created to be!"

Namaste'

Dr. Stacey A. Maxwell-Krockenberger

PROLOGUE

Lea

One thing that I really enjoy is spending time with my friends. When I was asked to meet them at a small Italian restaurant in the city, I was excited to go. I love the old neighborhood restaurants. You can find the most unbelievable homemade Italian food there. The smell of the fresh bread entices your taste buds. Avery and I jumped into the car and headed for South Philadelphia. It was a beautiful spring night, and I found the best parking spot, right down the street from the restaurant, which is never an easy thing.

We walked into the restaurant. It was the size of a row home, with just about twelve tables. The place was crowded and noisy. I looked around for my friends and found them sitting at a table in the corner. There were six people, and Avery and I brought the total to eight. All the women gathered at one end of the table while the men stayed together at the other end. We made our rounds by giving everyone a kiss hello. As I was working my way to an empty seat, I saw in my mind's eye, a man standing behind my friend, Lea. I poured a glass of red wine and tried to push the image of the man out of my head. He looked at me as if to ask, "Are you going to tell her that we are here?" Also coming into my view was a little girl holding a little boy's hand. I sat down at the table, just mildly entertained by my conversation with my friends. I was so distracted by the Spirits that I couldn't concentrate. I knew that he wasn't going to leave until I told her that they were all there. I looked across the table at my daughter, and shot her that familiar "I see dead people look". In turn, she shot back the "Please don't say anything look"! I was her mother and this of course could result in a "social embarrassment" to a teenager. At that age life is all about how you are perceived by others. So I tried my best to avoid the unavoidable.

After I finished my glass of wine, the pressure got to me and I blurted out in a whisper, "Lea, there is a man in spirit standing behind you. I also see a little boy too", Lea automatically thought of the little boy that she had lost during her pregnancy. Her eyes filled up with tears, but when I continued to tell her about the little girl whom I was seeing, Lea seemed puzzled. She knew nothing about a little girl's passing. "The man could be my father" she said. I was not aware that this was her father's old neighborhood, and that she herself had lived just around the corner with her parents years ago. Lea knew about my abilities, but never saw them in action, until now. Lea had received the most beautiful impromptu reading from her beloved father. He wanted her to know that he is sitting with her when she is talking to him in her car, while driving to work. It was important for him to validate that he does hear her. Her father also talked about his cooking and how he was so good at it. I relayed some memories so that they could reminisce a little bit about the old days. Lea shed tears of happiness and was filled with validation that left no doubt that this was her father. When she returned home, she spoke to her mother about the experience. Lea's mother was shocked and moved, to hear about her husband. But she was also pleasantly surprised to hear about the little girl, who could have been her daughter (Lea's sister), since she herself had also lost a child by miscarriage. Lea was not aware that the little girl whom I was seeing could have been her sister. It became abundantly clear to her that the spirits were trying to make her understand that they are all together and happy.

Of course, speaking to spirits was not always this way, and not always that simple. I had plenty of trials, heartache, confusion and misunderstandings along my journey.

PART ONE
MY CURSE

CHAPTER 1

MY EARLY YEARS

As defined by my mother, a "simpleton" is a person of simple mind, with a silly personality. This was the nickname that my mother gave to me. She admired my simple way of looking at life, my silliness, and my easy going personality. I was born the middle child of wonderful parents. I had loving grandparents and two awesome siblings. My sister, Anna is the oldest and my brother, Kevin, is the youngest. It's been said that the middle child needs to fight for attention. The first child is celebrated for her "firsts." The baby of the family is spoiled and everyone caters to the baby. Maybe that was the reason for my silly personality. Maybe I wanted and needed to get noticed. There were times when my parents would catch me talking into a mirror. My family would laugh at me, but I wasn't sure why. I didn't think that it was strange, because I thought that everyone did that. I would just turn and continue my conversation. In my mind, it was a two sided conversation. My mother would tell you that I was always a happy and sensitive child; a "joy" in her words.

The only oddity in my life was the fact that I had some mildly strange personality traits. As a young girl, I had an unusual ability to relate to people. I seemed to be able to say the right things to make people happy, and I was able to give profound advice. I believe that this was my empathic ability at work, enabling me to connect with the energy of others, and to take on their emotions as my own. I believe that this helped me to connect with them on a level that most people could not.

I also had pre-cognitive ability, which allowed me to know about an event before it actually occurred. Thoughts would come to me of a person to whom I had not spoken in a long time, and I would soon after run into them or receive a phone call from them. It happened so often that I thought it was normal and natural.

I was also prone to Lucid Dreaming, or out of body experiences (OBE). I called them frozen dreams or nightmares. I experienced visits from the spirits of loved ones and of people whom I did not know. My mind would be awake and aware, but my body would be in a "frozen" state, and unable to move. I would be scared and wanting to scream, and my mind would beg my body to move. But I could not move or speak a word, as spirits would sit on the end of my bed and try to communicate with me. The spirits' identities ranged from strangers to family members who had passed over.

I would ask my family and friends if they had ever experienced anything like this, and some said that they had, but most said they had not. These visions did not seem to be detrimental to me, so we chalked them up as dreams, and this was normal for 'Victoria".

I lived in a two bedroom home in South Philadelphia for the first part of my young childhood. My mom's parents lived only blocks away and my dad's mother lived around the corner. My dad's father, Kevin, had passed long before I was born, and I never met him physically. However, years later I met him in spirit and I have a very strong connection to him now. I went to Catholic schools and I enjoyed going to the parks and playing in the streets with my cousins. My sister and I would visit my grandmother frequently. During those visits, we would play waitress or drink tea, and discuss all of our pretend children and the problems that they were giving us. My grandmother enjoyed the visits and was happy to play along. We loved the band, THE MONKEES, and loved their TV show. We would pretend that they were our husbands. My sister, being the oldest, always got to pick first. She always got Davey Jones, because he was the cutest!

We spent summer weekends at my grandparents' home, at the South Jersey shore. My mom's parents were right out of a sitcom. They lived in the same physical dwelling, but they lived separate lives. My Mom-Mom would complain about Pop-Pop all the time. She complained that she had to always search his pockets for money, and that he was never home because he was out with his friends. Oddly enough, she always cooked for him, and had his clothes cleaned and pressed, and ready for him. This was how she showed her love for him. I'm sure that Pop-Pop had his issues with her too. I just didn't hear him complain so much, because I spent more time with Mom-Mom. Despite the bickering, it was entertaining, and we always had great summers. He was a carpenter, who worked very hard and never missed work. He always provided well for his family. He was jolly, and very loving to my mom, and to my siblings, and to me. But when he wasn't working, he liked to party with his friends. Mom-Mom and Pop-Pop were just "cut from a different cloth", as the saying goes.

By the time I was a teenager, we lived in South Jersey, only about twenty minutes from Philadelphia. I attended public school and had no problem making friends. My mother and grandmother would call me "Dear Abby", because I would come home to tell them the problems that my friends were having. They teased all the time, asking me why my friends would ask ME for advice, and what did I really know about life's trials and tribulations. I really didn't understand where I got this advice that I gave to my friends, but they seemed happy, and kept coming back for more. It seemed very out of character for me, because I never came across as a very thought provoking person, yet somehow it worked.

The time came for me to get my driver's license. I didn't have my own car yet, so I would drive my dad's big yellow station wagon. My friends and I called it the Banana Boat. One night my friends and I were out in the Banana Boat, and we were riding around town. I had the idea to play "Chinese Fire Drill." This is a game where as the car is stopped at a red light, everyone gets out and runs around the car and gets back into the car in a different seat. We did this, and we were laughing hysterically. It's was a dangerous game to be playing, because of course, someone could get hit by a car. On this particular night, we must have done this at five different red lights. The drivers around us in the other cars were not happy with us, but we were laughing too hysterically to notice. After the last light, I pulled the car into a McDonald's parking lot because we were going to get something to eat. I was still laughing so hard that my stomach was hurting. When we finally started to get out of the car, I looked to my left side, and there, sitting in the next car, was my dad in my mother's car. He had followed us from the last couple of lights, and very upset/angry that I could put my friends in danger like that.

I was told to go straight home. I knew that I was in so much trouble, and so did my friends. My best friend, Kasey, was the only one who would come into the house with me to face the music. For someone who gave such good and grounding advice to people, I had made some stupid choices. Needless to say, I was punished that night.

I met Frank during the summer of 1984. We met in Wildwood, New Jersey. I was now working summer jobs there, and staying with Mom-Mom. Frank was doing the same thing, and spending the summers there with his mom and brothers. His cousin, Dana, and I were friends, and she introduced us. It wasn't love at first sight. We became friends and we would all hang out together, in a big group of guys and girls. We hung out on the beach during the day, and on the boardwalk at night. The more time we spent together, the closer we became. Our friendship grew into love.

I remember falling in love with his ability to command respect from all of his friends. They didn't make a move without first asking Frank what he wanted to do. I guess that I admired that quality in him. Frank also had a bit of a bad boy edge, which appealed to me as well. I was also attracted to his serious and quiet personality. These were traits which were the complete opposite of my silly and rather loud self. I remember this period as one of the best times of my life. The smell of suntan lotion and pizza, and the sound of the boardwalk rides whipping through the air, and the tram car cruising down the boardwalk, still bring a smile to my face.

Frank and I continued to date for a number of years. We shared many holidays together as well as many milestones in our lives. We went to each other's senior proms, attended each other's graduations, and were together when we started new jobs. Our lives seemed to mold together very nicely. His family loved me and welcomed me into their home like a daughter. Since Frank had three brothers, they were happy to have a girl in the family. My family embraced Frank as well. My brother, Kevin, was especially happy to have Frank in the family. He grew up with two sisters. Anne already had a great husband, Gary. And now, with Frank and his three brothers, Kevin would have a "guy" family. Frank's family and my family got along so well. Frank and I had many good times, especially during the summers at the shore, with both families. It was very unique and special to have both of our families wanting to spend time with each other.

Frank and I had been dating for eight years, when he finally proposed. I was very excited when that moment had finally come. It was Christmas Eve, and it was our tradition to exchange gifts on that night. I knew that he would propose soon. I had joked with him that if he didn't propose soon, there would be trouble in paradise. Frank was always looking for the perfect time to do things. He wanted to wait until he graduated from college. Then he wanted to wait until we were financially stable.

Once we became engaged, we were busy planning a wedding and looking forward to buying our first home. My life was falling into place nicely. We agreed that having children was important to both of us. In my mind, I couldn't think of anything but my bright future. My dreams of having a husband, of having a home with a white picket fence, and of starting a family, were coming true. I thought how wonderful it would be to see my tummy grow, and to feel life growing inside of me. I daydreamed about what our children would look like and what we would name them. I even daydreamed about my baby's nursery, and how it would look.

At this point, my sister, Anne, and my best friend Kasey, who had already married Frank's brother, Angelo, each had two children. I was the godmother to one child for each of them. I loved these kids and couldn't wait to give them cousins.

CHAPTER 2
THE "CURSE" BEGINS

It was the spring of 1994, and I had been married to my high school sweetheart for two and a half years. This was a happy time for me. Frank and I had bought a house and we were fixing it up and making it a home. My life was falling into place. We began to discuss starting a family. I was twenty-eight years old and Frank was twenty-seven.

As I began the next chapter in my life, some of my very good friends were doing the same. There were so many exciting things going on. Kasey and Angelo had twin boys. Another very close friend, Monica, was getting married, and we were planning all the parties and festivities that go along with weddings. Kasey and I were both to be bridesmaids in Monica's wedding party. Frank and Angelo were also in the wedding party. Monica and her future husband, Angelo and Kasey, and Frank and I, were all very good friends, and had spent a lot of time together. We had many dinner dates, spent vacations together, and just hung out at each other's houses. We were together every weekend. We always had a good time.

The month before the wedding, Frank wasn't feeling well. He was feeling dizzy and light headed and was having heart palpitations. He was beginning to feel this way quite often, and we finally went to our family doctor to try to get some answers. Our doctor told us that it could be anything from cancer to diabetes. We began seeing different specialists and having all sorts of tests done. Everything from routine blood work to CT scans to ultrasounds were done. It seemed that we were going to a different doctor, or for a different test, every week.

After seeing several specialists, we were not getting the answers that we felt we needed. Frank was still feeling ill, and I was determined to find out what was wrong with him. We became obsessed with his illness. I was becoming convinced that he would be seriously ill or perhaps die. What would I do if he never got better? What would I do if he died? How would I go on? I cried just about every day out of worry. We were too young to have these worries and fears.

Frank and I were still going through all of this when Monica's wedding day had arrived. Finally, I thought, we would have something joyful and fun to take my attention away from our problems. On the morning of the wedding, Kasey and I took our dresses over to Monica's house to meet the other girls in the bridal party. The plan was for all of the bridesmaids to get dressed there and wait for the photographer and limo. When we got there, everyone was excited. There was a lot of confusion, having so many girls getting dressed in one tiny house. Monica's parents' house was small, with only one bathroom. The bridesmaids all dressed and got ready in Monica's bedroom, while Monica got dressed in her mother's bedroom. This is a custom that many brides follow on their wedding day.

After all of the bridesmaids were dressed, we came out of the bedroom and the photographer began taking our pictures while we were waiting for Monica to emerge. Our bridesmaids' dresses were the style for that time period. The dresses were fuchsia colored and the tops had lots of ruffles, and were off the shoulders. The dresses were floor length and our shoes had been dyed to perfectly match the color of the gowns.

Finally, the door to Monica's mom's bedroom opened and a beautiful princess emerged. Monica was stunning and she smiled from ear to ear. Her face was glowing and her eyes were sparkling. Her make-up was perfect. She had naturally dark, curly, hair and her hair was up off of her face and there were some loose curls cascading down onto her face. She wore a traditional white bridal gown, with a full skirt and a long train. The gown had a lot of beadwork and appliqués. Monica's happiness was evident in her face. This day was a long time coming. The wedding had been postponed six months before. All of the bridesmaids were happy that this day had finally come for Monica.

The photographer began taking more pictures. All the traditional pictures were taken. There was one of the bride with her dad looking into his baby girl's eyes. There was one with her mom fixing her veil. And there was one with the bridesmaids surrounding her, and admiring her beauty. In the midst of all this excitement, there was a knock at the door. Someone answered the door, and standing in the doorway were two women who were friends of the groom's mother. When Monica saw them, she knew that something was wrong. We all did.

The women came in, and Monica started to ask, in a very worried voice, what was wrong. They explained that there had been a car accident and that the groom was in the hospital. Monica started to scream, "NO!" Over and over she said that word. Each time she said it, she got louder. Tears filled her eyes as she screamed. She was told that he was okay, but needed to be checked out because he had hit a tree with his car.

Monica demanded to be taken to the hospital at that instant. Her father tried calming her down but there was no calming her. "Monica," he said. "Calm down. Take a deep breath and let's think this through." Her mother brought her a glass of water and tried to make her sit down. The bridesmaids were in disbelief. We didn't know what to do. No matter what anyone said to her, Monica was not listening. She stared at nothing and looked like she was in a state of shock. After a few minutes went by, she turned to her father and said that she was going to the hospital. And out the door she went to the waiting limousine. She instructed the driver to take her to the hospital. She needed to see him. She was taken to the hospital in her wedding gown.

The bridesmaids, her parents, her brother, and the two other women who had come over with the news, were left at the house. Monica's dad asked the bridesmaids to go to the church to stall the priest and the arriving guests.

Naturally, when we arrived at the Church, the guests were already arriving. We did our best to explain the situation to the guests. It was very difficult because we didn't know what would happen. I remember being very optimistic, and thinking that the bride and groom would soon be there, and that all of this would be over. We would just begin the ceremony as planned, and then move on to the reception.

We were probably at the church for an hour and a half, before it was decided that the wedding wasn't going to take place on that day. It was like a scene from a movie. Everyone was in disbelief. If I had not been part of this drama, I would never have believed it.

Monica's wedding never took place. She had learned that the accident was just a fender bender. Her fiancé had been getting second thoughts about the marriage and decided not to go through with it. Monica was literally left at the altar. Her life fell apart right in front of everyone. Needless to say, she was a mess for a very long time. I needed to help her through this. She was my friend and she needed me. I was already an emotional mess from everything that I had been going through with Frank. I was trying to take care of him and to keep up his spirit. Now I felt that I needed to take care of Monica, too.

There were many days over the next few months, when I would go to Monica's house in the morning. She was living by herself in the home that she was to share with her husband. I would encourage her to get out of bed and to eat. She was fading away mentally and physically. She would try her best, but she was embarrassed and distraught. She had so many questions, but I had no answers for her. I felt so helpless. The only thing that I could do was to be her shoulder to cry on.

After work on many evenings, I would stop at Monica's house to check on her before I went home. I would try to console her and comfort her. My heart broke for her, and it was very emotionally draining.

I would go home to Frank, who was still sick and seemed to be getting worse. He was depressed and tired of not feeling well. We still were not getting answers. I continued to do my own research. I came up with many diagnoses for what was ailing Frank. None of them were good.

I was now consumed with the depression and anxiety from Frank's and Monica's situations. The month following Monica's wedding date had gotten worse and more intense. We still had no answers on Frank's health. Monica's depression was increasing. I was running on empty. All I could feel was sadness, hopelessness, and helplessness.

What I did not know, was how fast the table was going to turn, and that I would be the one who would be looking for solace. I do not blame the next events in my life on Frank or Monica, or on the difficulties that had beset them. The events that took place were the start of my learning about my empathetic gifts, and the journey that is now changing my life.

CHAPTER 3
ALMOST PREGNANT

We were getting some positive news about Frank's illness, and it seemed as though his condition was improving. It was Labor Day, and we were spending the Holiday weekend at the Jersey Shore. Frank's parents owned a beautiful summer home there, and all of Frank's brothers and their families, were there at the house. The house was in the family for about twenty years, and Frank and his brothers spent summers there when they were kids. When we got married, we spent every weekend there, and had lots of fun with the family and neighbors on the block. At the end of the street, there was a lake, which fed into the canal, and eventually fed into the ocean. The family owned a boat and jet skis, and we were on the water all the time.

One Saturday night, I woke up suddenly and was feeling very uneasy. The only word that I could find to describe my feeling was "gloom". I had never felt this way before. Although there were about seven other people in the house that night, I felt very alone. Anxiety passed through my entire body like a raging hot flash. I was light headed and nauseous, and I had an unstoppable urge to breakdown and cry. My whole body was shaking. I shook as if I had awakened abruptly from a horrible nightmare. I was trying to get my mind focused again. I woke Frank for comfort. Even though he held me and tried to calm me, my emotions were too strong. When Frank was unable to help me, I began to wake up his brothers one by one, to ask them to talk to me. They tried their best to help, but to no avail.

The week continued with my odd emotional state and anxiety. I was not sleeping much, and was eating very little. I turned to my parents and my brother, Kevin, and my sister, Anne, for guidance and help. My family felt that I was too wrapped up in trying to fix everyone's problems. I was focusing too much of my energy on negativity, and it was bringing me down. In my own mind, I felt that once I fixed everyone's problems, I would begin to feel better. This pattern of not eating and not sleeping continued much into the following weeks. Very often I would have hot flashes. I began to figure out that these hot flashes were the anxiety that I was experiencing.

One morning, I was in a meeting at work, with seven of my co-workers and my boss. We were going over the new marketing plan for the company. As the meeting progressed, I had the feeling of heat coming over me. The heat raced up my back to my neck, and then to the top of my head, and finally to my face. My heart started pounding out of my chest. I began to feel short of breath. I was getting scared. I looked up at the clock on the wall. I watched the second hand tick. The seconds were turning into minutes, but it seemed like it was taking forever for time to go by, and for the meeting to end. I got up and excused myself from the meeting, because I knew that I could no longer sit there. I wanted and needed to get to a hospital. Frank was at work in King of Prussia, Pennsylvania, which was at least forty-five minutes away. I needed to go to the hospital now. I picked up the phone and called Kasey. Kasey left work immediately, and came to pick me up from my office. When we got to the hospital, Kasey told the front desk that I was having a heart attack. Immediately, I was taken back and seen by the doctors and nurses. They checked my vital signs, and determined that I was stable. They began checking my blood work. Once things calmed down, Kasey called Frank and my parents, and tried to explain to them what was going on.

We waited patiently for some answers. I began to calm down, and was resting. I was comforted in knowing that I may finally get some help. About an hour had passed, when a male nurse pulled back the curtain and stated that he had some results from the blood work. His face looked a bit puzzled as he told us that I was "almost pregnant." Kasey and I looked at each other and then Kasey turned and said, "WHAT?? I never heard of such a thing. Either you are pregnant or you are not pregnant!" The expression on nurse's face was priceless, as he absorbed Kasey's statement. He said, "Well, it's a very light pink line, but it is there."

A mixture of emotions took over my body. I was surprised, happy, and anxious, all at the same time. "This is great news!" Kasey said to me. "Yes, it is", I responded. I thought to myself that this was probably why I have been feeling so emotional. My hormones were going a little crazy inside of me. Now all of that will end. Little did I know at the time, that this was only the beginning of a harder road for me. The beginning of what should have been a beautiful time in my life was actually the beginning of one of the worst times in my life. The beauty of becoming a mother for the first time, and the happiness that goes with it, would be taken from me. I would never FEEL the happiness of telling my friends and family. I would never FEEL the excitement of decorating the baby's room. I would not experience the surprise and joy of a baby shower. I was completely incapable of any happiness for the next ten months. In place of those emotions, stood depression, fear, loneliness and shame. This, by far, would be the worst experience of my life.

CHAPTER 4

JUST HORMONES

As my pregnancy progressed, I tried to put on a happy face. This pregnancy was something that Frank and I wanted and had planned for. Therefore, I should have been elated and excited. Instead, all I could focus on was how I could feel better emotionally, and how I could fix myself. My family and friends said that I needed to stop my emotional breakdowns, and just get happy. The people closest to me could not understand what I was going through. They could not comprehend how I could be so depressed during such a happy time. They were very concerned about my mental state. The ironic thing was that because I was pregnant, my family thought, just as I had thought, that the reason that I was feeling so down was because of my hormones. I tried to put my mind at ease with that same reasoning. However, no one I knew had ever experienced this level of depression during a pregnancy. As most people know, this is a common experience after giving birth, but not before.

I felt that I needed medication and that I needed to see a doctor. I wanted to see a psychologist and not a psychiatrist, because in my mind, seeing a psychiatrist meant that I was crazy. Although I refused to admit to anyone that I could be crazy, in secret, I did believe that I might be going crazy. And seeing a psychiatrist would confirm that in fact, maybe I was crazy. I also knew that a psychiatrist may suggest medication, and I was unwilling to take any medication for fear that I would harm my baby. I did not want to unintentionally harm the baby.

One night, I woke up in a cold sweat, depressed and exhausted. A few weeks had gone by without sleeping well or eating much. I was not myself. I sat up in bed and was full of emotions. I looked over at Frank, who was sleeping so peacefully. He was lying on his side, curled up with the comforter from our bed entwined in his arms. I could see him breathing as I watched the comforter move slightly up, and then down, with every breath that he took. I actually was jealous that he was so peaceful. Then I became very angry with him. I thought to myself, "How dare he lay there and sleep without a care or worry! Doesn't he know how I feel? Doesn't he care?"

I stumbled out of bed and lost my balance. I was feeling dizzy. I decided to go downstairs and get something to drink. As I approached the steps, I stood there thinking how easy it would be to throw myself down the steps and lose the baby. In my mind, if I lost the baby accidentally, I could then take medication, and I could feel myself again. I would be cured, and then I could try for another baby when I felt better. No one would ever know that I did it on purpose. No one would ever think that I was so desperate.

The next thought that came into my mind was what stopped me. "God would know that I intentionally hurt myself and killed my baby". I would actually be murdering my baby. I knew that it was against the law of God to take the life of another. My punishment for this would be to go to Hell and live in eternal damnation. It may look like an accident to everyone, but God would know that it was not. This fetus growing inside of me was a life. It was a life, even though it was not breathing the same air that I was breathing. I knew that Hell existed, because I was living in it now to some degree. Being in Hell for all eternity would be unbearable. It was in this moment that I knew that the anguish that I was experiencing was my cross to bear, and that I needed to carry this pregnancy to the best of my ability.

CHAPTER 5
NINE MONTHS AND COUNTING

My mother spent countless mornings coaxing me to get out of bed. Frank spent countless hours at night lying awake, trying to comfort me. My friends, Monica and Kasey, would come for visits to make me laugh and take me out. Even my seven year old niece, Brigette, was told by my sister to cheer me up. I really believe that the people who loved me the most would have suffered greatly if they didn't believe that my hormones were doing this to me. They needed to believe this. But I did not believe it.

My doctors told me that this was relatively normal, and that I needed to learn coping skills. I learned the rubber band trick for negative thoughts. I placed a rubber band on my wrist and snapped it every time a negative thought came into my mind. That was supposed to "snap" me out of the negativity. I learned to eat healthful foods, to exercise, to practice yoga, to use positive affirmations, and to use sound soothing meditations. No matter what I did to try and help myself, nothing worked for very long.

I began to feel sorry for myself. My Catholic faith was being tested. Why would God let a pregnant woman have this cross to bear? In my mind, I was the only one who could help, and I was on my own. I should have been spending time looking at baby names and baby clothes and enjoying this magical time in my life. But instead, I spent hours researching my condition. I did a lot of research and could not find any case where another pregnant woman felt as bad, emotionally, as I did. I knew that if I could only take anxiety medication, I would feel better.

There were many nights when I could not sleep. I would drink herbal tea and read self-help books. The scary and negative thoughts would always find a way to take over my mind.

I would often wake up in the middle of the night. I would tell myself that I was OK, and that I didn't need a lot of sleep. I would hop from one bed to another bed in my house, or from one sofa to another sofa, hoping that I would find a spot with "magical energy", which would allow me to sleep.

There was one night in particular, when I decided that I needed to go for a walk. I thought that being out in the night air would help me sleep. I put on a jacket over my night gown and slipped on a pair of shoes. I tried to open my front door quietly, so that I wouldn't wake Frank. I stepped out into the darkness. The air was cool and clean. The stars were bright and the moon was full. It was 2:00 am and there was not a soul around. I walked for blocks with only a few street lights. My intention was to feel better, but instead, I started to cry. I could not understand what God was thinking, and what His plan was for me. I had faith in God, and that was the only thing that I could cling to for the little bit of sanity that I had left. I knew that I needed to be strong, and to put one foot in front of the other, and keep going.

I was still working at this point, and I was grateful for my job. Work was a safe place for me. I knew that I had to stay in control when I was there, and that I could not spiral downward. For this reason, I was happy and relieved to go to work every day.

As my depression grew, so did my belly. The baby who was living inside of me began to move and kick and make herself known. I was feeling relieved to know that this would all be over soon. When this pregnancy was over, I knew that

I could get the medication that I needed. The thought of this hell being over gave me some happiness. Knowing that the baby was healthy gave me some happiness as well, but that was a second thought. I know that this sounds crazy now, but it was my reality.

I was in my eighth month of pregnancy, and we were going to birthing classes every week. This totally stressed me out. As the time got closer to giving birth, I was stressed by the idea of taking care of the baby. How was I going to care for this child if I could not care for myself? What if I turned into one of those mothers who hurt their child after they gave birth? This started a whole new worry that I had not had before. All sense of reason was lost. I was now obsessed with worrying about worrying that I would harm my child.

I agreed to let Frank take me to a psychiatrist. I had made up my mind that if I trusted and believed the doctor, and he recommended medication, I would take what was prescribed. I knew in my heart that this was my last chance to get help. The thought of hurting my child was too much for me to take. I told myself that if I could not get the help that I needed, I would take my own life, before I would harm my child. She would be better off without me, anyway.

The doctor did prescribe medication. It was a form of Xanax. After taking the medication, I did experience some relief. However, the bad thoughts did not stop completely. My mind was so conditioned to the negative thoughts that my body would experience negative physical reactions, such as nausea and headaches before I even realized that these thoughts had manifested. The only thing that I could do was to pray and to wait for the baby to arrive.

Finally, the long-awaited day had come. Delivering my daughter was a wonderful experience, partly because I was so happy to have the pregnancy behind me, and partly because it was such an easy birth. She came so easily and so quickly. She was beautiful, and she was perfect in every way. I felt so blessed.

As the weeks and months went on, I was able to get the help that I needed. My life began to return to normal, or at least to my "new" normal. I was a new mom and was so happy to be able to enjoy this time, and my new baby.

CHAPTER 6
GOING INTO BUSINESS

Frank and I were about to embark on a new adventure when 2001 rolled around. By this time, I had my second child, a son named Anthony. I had left my full time job, and had become a stay at home mom for about four years at this point. I enjoyed being at home and raising my children full time.

Frank, who is a passionate entrepreneur, had been researching several business opportunities for us to pursue. After discussing all of our options, we decided to open an early childhood learning center franchise, with a company which was known nationwide. This seemed like the perfect opportunity for us, as our children were young and could attend the school. Avery was five and Anthony was three.

The plan was for me to be the on-site owner, and the children would attend the school and still be with me.

This was a huge undertaking and I was scared. My role at the school would be to give tours and to market the school. Although my work experience was in marketing and advertising, I had no experience in managing a staff or running a business. I was not at all confident that I could make this business work. We would be required to assume a huge financial debt, and I felt that the weight was on my shoulders for the business to be successful. Even though I was worried and nervous about it, part of me was excited for the adventure. I also knew that this was a very good opportunity and that it was too good to pass up. Frank kept giving me encouragement, and assured me that he would be by my side. He also made the promise that once the business was up and running, and we were able to make a living from it, he would quit his full time job and take over management of the center. Then I could go back to being a full time mom.

When the school finally opened, I began my new role as the on-site owner. In this role, I would give tours to perspective families and register them if they wanted their children to attend. This job required meeting and talking with many new people. I had always been comfortable talking to people. I was, and still am, a very sociable person. I was taken off guard when I started to notice that as I was giving tours to perspective families, I would begin to get feelings of apprehension, nervousness and even some fear.

I began to understand that I wasn't nervous about talking and meeting the families. I realized that I was feeling the emotions that the parents had been feeling over leaving their children in a new environment, and in the care of strangers. It felt like I was leaving my own child. I decided that this was because I was a parent, and could place myself in their position.

After everything I've learned about myself, I now know that this was my empathetic ability to feel their emotions. It was a curse and a blessing because I had the empathy to console their true fears, even if they didn't tell me. However, as a business person, it was my job to "close" the deal, and I felt that I couldn't do that because of the anguish that I was feeling over their decision. I knew that this was the best choice for the children all around, but yet I felt that I needed to stop short of really selling them on the idea that they should enroll their children. They needed to come to this decision on their own without me pushing them.

Frank often "coached" me about how to make the parents understand what they would lose by not signing up that day. The thought of putting that pressure on them made me feel very uncomfortable. I had to do it my way in order for it to work for me.

I managed to fill the school after two years in business, and felt great about this accomplishment. I had learned a lot in the two years. About a month before we opened for business, we needed had to hire a Director for the school. This would be the person who would take charge of the day to day operations, including staffing and education of the children. The person we hired had several years of experience and came from another school with high recommendations.

I was fortunate enough to hire Jean. Jean was a wonderful Director and she had the school's best interest as her priority. She taught me so much about managing the school. To this day, I credit her with teaching me how to run the school. Because of her, I was able to run the business end of things beautifully. To add to my staff, Jean and I hired an Assistant Director, Catherine.

Jean, Catherine and I got along so well! We made a great trio and we would laugh all the time. I enjoyed going to work because I felt like I was spending time with my girlfriends. When I originally hired Jean, she told me that she would only be staying with me for three years. Her intention was to stay until her son reached school age, and then she wanted to move on to other things. Her son attended our school and that made it convenient for her, since he was with her all day. However, she ended up staying on with me for five years.

Every year, our company holds a convention for all the owners of the franchises throughout the nation. In 2005, Frank and I won a very prestigious award. This award was quite an honor, and it was the reward that we received for all our efforts. Of course, I could not have accomplished this award without my amazing Director and Assistant Director. I was so excited to share the news with them and to start planning changes and improvements, with the intention of winning this award again the next year. I returned from the convention with fresh ideas and success stories to share with Jean and Catherine.

As soon as we returned, Jean asked to have a meeting with Frank and me. During the meeting, she told us that she had taken another job and would be leaving in two weeks. I thought that she was kidding. She assured me that she was not joking, and to say that I was floored would definitely be an understatement. Jean was very surprised that I was so shocked. She thought that I had suspected that she was looking for another job. She had been interviewing before we left for the convention.

After the meeting with Jean, I called Catherine into my office to share the news with her. She was completely shocked. She had no idea that this was coming. This was upsetting to both of us because we were all so close. The relationship between the three of us went way beyond a work relationship. We attended each other's holiday events, children's parties, graduations, Communions. We cried on each other's shoulders. I even spent a night in the hospital with Jean when she fell ill.

As devastating as this news was to us, it would be worse for the staff and the parents and children who loved the team that we had built. Everyone was comfortable with this team, which was why the school had been so successful. As upsetting as this was, I knew deep down in my heart that Jean needed to move on. She had told me that from the beginning. I needed to do what was best for me and for my school. I immediately began sending Catherine to Director's training, and occupied myself with the task of finding a new Assistant Director.

With the news that Jean was leaving, emotions began to rise for everyone involved with the school. Teachers were upset because they didn't know what to expect from Catherine as their new boss. They worried that they may be moved around into new positions, or that they would be let go. Parents worried that the quality of the program would change with a new Director. Catherine was completely stressed over the responsibility that she would assume. Jean had full control over the school, and Catherine had been allowed only a limited amount of responsibility. The anxiety was palpable and it was coming from all directions. I was feeling very anxious and couldn't stop moving or doing something to keep my mind occupied. I was full of nervous energy and couldn't relax. This was not a normal feeling for me. I was, and still am, usually a very calm and happy person, and I know that things always work out. "Don't worry, be happy", as the song goes. I was giving pep talks, and trying to reassure everyone that things would be fine. It would be business as usual. What I realized later, was that I was beginning to feel the emotions of everyone in the school and it was becoming overwhelming.

One morning, I woke up with the same feeling of doom that I had felt so many years earlier. It was that horrible feeling of dread, and it made me nauseous and it made my stomach turn. Instantly, panic came over me as I remembered what I had gone through so many years before. This cannot be happening to me again. Jean's leaving was not the end of the world. I was feeling the universal emotions that everyone at the school had been feeling but magnified tenfold. I was consoling them all just the day before. "Get a grip!" I thought to myself. I knew that I needed to call my doctor for an appointment and medication before this got out of control. But I was not sure how long it would take for the medication to work, and that compounded my anxiety. I was scared to death. I had too many responsibilities now. This was different than last time. I now had two children, a husband, and a business to run. I was feeling ashamed. I did not want to get sick again. What will people think if I fall apart? I needed to pull myself together because there were so many people who depended on me. As the days passed, I worried more and felt sicker. I began telling my family and friends what was happening. They were more concerned this time, and I could feel that. The last time this happened I was pregnant, and everyone assumed that it was my hormones that were out of control and causing my anxiety and depression. They could understand then, that there was a physical reason for me to feel sick. But this time there was no reason, and it was very hard to understand.

I couldn't understand it either. How could I be so upset over my Director leaving? This was a question that was posed by those close to me. I did not have an answer. I wished that I did. All I knew was that I was spiraling out of control again. I knew that I could not go through this again. I carried this cross years ago. Why am I doing it again? The medication was not helping. It wasn't even taking the edge off my anxiety. The depression was taking hold of me. I could not bear to see anyone at work. I tried to act normal, but I would have frequent breakdowns. I drove in my car for hours, just so I could cry and no one would see how bad I really was. I just wanted to escape my mind.

I felt so guilty for feeling this way, and for how it was affecting my family and friends. I tried to rationalize with myself and to figure out what would help me. I told myself that Frank would have to quit his job and take over running the school. I could not handle it anymore. I felt so trapped. I couldn't eat. I could hardly sleep. I needed to medicate myself to sleep for just a few hours. When I had to watch my kids at their sporting events, I did my best to look interested, but it was so difficult to concentrate. I was mentally absent at family gatherings. I always looked like I was in a different world. The only thing that gave me peace was seeing my psychiatrist. I was now seeing him every week. I told him that I didn't understand why I was going through this anguish again. He explained to me that some people just have anxiety and panic attacks for no discernible reason. That answer did not sit well with me.

After a few weeks of this downward spiral, I was at my parents' house and I simply collapsed in their bed. I called my doctor and begged him to put me away into a mental hospital. He did not think that was the right decision for me. He knew that I had unconditional love and support from my parents, Frank and the kids. He told me that I would be okay. I was not so sure of that. That evening, Frank and the children came to take me home. I physically could not move from my parents' bed. I was so detached from everyone, including my Frank and my own children. I refused to go home. I knew that I was upsetting them, but I was absent of any emotion. I did not care and I was trapped in my own head. I did not have the ability to care about their feelings. I had no plans to return home. I told Frank that he had to get the kids off to school the next morning. It was very difficult for me to say this, but I could not help it. That evening, Frank had to explain to my nine year old daughter and my seven year old son why I wasn't coming home. He told them that I loved them, but that I was sick, and that I may not be seeing them for a while. He broke down in tears in front of them. My children still remember trying to console their dad that night. They remember everything about that moment, and they remember that it was the worst time of their lives.

I couldn't help thinking that I was being punished or cursed for some reason. After all, I was a good person. I believed in God and knew that He loved me. I could not be angry with God, I told myself. I knew that I needed to accept what was happening, and the sooner that I accepted it, the better off I would be, mentally and physically.

Slowly, the medication that I was prescribed started to work. I went home after about a week. I took some time off from work, and rested. I began to climb out of the hole that I was in. Frank started to work from home, and this was a Godsend. I got back to work and slowly I started to feel better. After four months, I was back to feeling normal again. During that time, Catherine took over as Director of the school and everything fell into place nicely.

My children were finding new hobbies and activities and they each had a very busy social life. I was beginning to enjoy going to their events, and I was starting to be happy and to enjoy my life again. I was so happy to have gotten past this hurdle again. My hell was over and behind me. Or so I thought.

CHAPTER 7
THIRD AND FINAL

Life was wonderful for me and for my family. Avery was in high school. She was enjoying her high school experience. She had plenty of friends, and she was a cheerleader. Anthony was in middle school. He loves sports, and was busy playing basketball and baseball. In the summer, he loved to surf in the ocean as we spent our weekends at the family shore home.

In the fall and spring we were spending weekends on the sports fields as a family. Week nights we spent in our car running from one practice to another. It was a crazy lifestyle and not your "Leave it to Beaver" home with dinner on the table at 5:00pm every night, but we loved it. These are some of my best memories, and I will always hold these memories in my heart and treasure them.

Our business was running well and was in good hands with our Director, Catherine, and Assistant Director, Isabel. I was able to take a step back, and not spend nine hours a day there, as I had done in the past. I was spending more time at home with my family.

Although everything and everyone in my life was doing well, I began to notice that I was becoming emotional again. People would tell me stories about their personal lives, and I could feel the pain, the hurt, or the joy of their situations. To some extent, I know that this is normal. Most people would feel upset if they were told about a distressful situation, even if it did not involve them personally. Most human beings are born with some level of empathy, and can feel sorrow or joy at the pain or happiness of others. But mine was deeper. I felt the emotion and it stayed with me.

I would feel the emotions physically, too. It was not uncommon for me to walk into the infant room and hear a baby crying and have my breasts begin to lactate. This had happened to me years prior, when my niece would cry. However, my own daughter was only a year old at the time, and I just figured that it was still my hormones from childbirth. Sometimes I would hold a baby, and say that my uterus was pounding, as a joke. But the truth was that I would really feel a sensation in my stomach.

I love to "people watch", and on occasion, while having dinner with friends in restaurants, I would feel like I was "reading" other patrons in the restaurant. I would tell my companions a detailed story about the person across the room. It was entertainment to us. We would laugh it off, and my friends or family would jokingly tell me that I was nuts.

There were other times when I would be in a public place, such as a restaurant, store, casino, or basically anyplace where a lot of people were gathered, and I would feel panic or worry. I would have to get up and leave. It was easy to deal with for the most part, because I would just physically remove myself from whatever was happening. I did not think that I was the only one who felt these things.

One night, I was lying in bed saying my prayers, as I did every night. I told God how happy I was with my life and I thanked Him for everything that I had. The one thing that I had asked Him for was to be kept safe, and free of worry and depression. I explained to God that there was really nothing else that I wanted in life, except to never experience anything like that again. This seemed like a reasonable request. Exactly one week from the day that I said that prayer, all hell broke loose again.

My family, my parents, my siblings, and their families, had planned to take a long weekend trip to the Pocono Mountains. My parents rented a beautiful home for us to occupy, and we were excited to spend the time together. My mom and I had gone up first with my kids. We wanted to get an early start on the weekend so that we would not need to rush. We thought that we could take our time, have a nice dinner, and then relax while we waited for the rest of the family to get there. We unpacked at the house that we had rented, and got settled. Then we ventured out to get some dinner.

We found a very nice restaurant at the top of one of the ski slopes. It had windows all around so that you could watch the skiers. It was night time, but the slopes were lit up like a Christmas tree, and people were still skiing. The lights made the snow glisten. It was truly a beautiful sight. But from the time that I walked into the restaurant, I had an uneasy feeling. Of course, I tried to ignore it. We were shown to our table and began looking at the menu. I was beginning to get a knot in my stomach. I felt my body getting warm, and I was starting to breathe heavier. All of a sudden it came over me like a tidal wave. I was hit head on with a panic attack. I had to get out of that restaurant. With no explanation to my mom and kids, I got up and practically ran out of the restaurant.

I got outside into the cold night air. I was hoping that breathing in that air would help relieve my attack. I was pacing back and forth, waiting for the relief. I called Frank from my cell phone and told him that I needed him. I told him to hurry! This was a bad one. He was on his way, and trying to get there as fast as possible. My sister, Anne, arrived at the restaurant and saw me outside. She was confused at first, but after only a few minutes, she knew what was happening. Unfortunately, everyone close to me was now familiar with these episodes. Anne took me into the ladies room and tried to calm me down. I was a bundle of nerves and she felt helpless. I could feel her heart breaking for me, and in turn, my heart was breaking for her. I was beginning to understand that when I was in this state, I was more sensitive to other people's emotions. I was also angry with myself. I hated putting other people through my pain, and I could see the helplessness and pain in my sister's eyes. Being the big sister she had always felt protective toward Kevin and me. This was devastating to her because she could do nothing to take this away from me. I knew that I needed to be alone, but I also knew that I needed Frank, and I felt like I was going out of my mind.

Anne managed to get me back to the house and up to my bedroom. I took medication to help me relax, and I got into bed and under the blankets, and I waited for Frank to come. I thought that when he got there, I would feel better, and this episode would pass. After what seemed like forever, Frank arrived. He slipped into the bed to hold me and try to comfort me. I felt some comfort in having him with me, but my anxiety did not go away. My body was trembling, with frequent hot flashes that would surge through my body starting at the top of my head and then dropping downward to my legs. The familiar nausea and stomach discomfort were next to invade my body that night. In fact, for the next four months, these physical symptoms would continue, and I was in my living hell again.

By this point, I had a lot of experience with these bouts of depression, anxiety and loneliness. I knew that the more I became upset, the harder it would be on my body. I knew that I needed to try to stay as calm as possible. If I couldn't control it, my body would also experience insomnia and involuntary body twitching, due to my body being so tense for an extended period of time. As much as I tried to stay under control, I could not. I was screaming for help inside. I did not have the power to fight this. I felt myself begin to make that downward spiral into the all too familiar dark place, which I knew as depression.

I asked myself over and over, "What the HELL??? Why me? Why again???" And once again, I found myself at my psychiatrist's office asking the same questions. Although I was so grateful for my doctor, and I felt that he had helped save my life, he was not helping me to understand why I keep going through this. Everything in my life was going perfectly. I could not and would not accept the fact that this would continue to keep happening for my entire life. This was NOT okay with me. This was not the real ME!

When I returned to work, I shared with Catherine and Isabel that I was once again going through this. They were both so good with me. They took over some of my work because I did not have the mindset to handle it myself. Catherine had been through this with me before, but this was all new to Isabel. Catherine had a deep belief in God, as did I. However, we practiced our faiths differently. She introduced me to her Church and her way of worship. Through her and her Church, I learned to read the Bible every morning, and to find the true meaning in the bible stories. This was life-changing for me, and I realized that God wasn't finished with me yet.

I truly believe that God puts people in our path who are placed here to help us along the road of life. I read years later in a book that we make a contract in Heaven and ask to have these experiences, so that our souls can evolve and ascend higher in the afterlife. This contract is designed around the goals that we choose to meet in the new life, into which we are about to be born. When designing this plan, we contract people to help us with our life's lessons. Their job is to "bump" us or "nudge" us in the right direction. I feel that Catherine was one of those people.

I believed that I was doing everything possible to help myself. I was praying, eating healthy, and exercising. The depression still held on, and there were times when I could not get out of bed. Avery would spend night after night in my bed with me, talking to me and rubbing my back. I could only imagine the fear that she felt, at the prospect of losing me again. Avery would get me out of bed, help me to get dressed, and brush my hair. These were all things that a seventeen year old girl should not need to do for her parent. I am so grateful for her love and understanding. One night she convinced me to have dinner at a friends' house. She told me that it would be good for me and that I needed to go.

I managed to pull myself together and go to the dinner party with Frank. I went, and sat at the table with the strangest feeling. I was unable to interact in the conversation with all of my friends. I did not want them to know that I was in this same dark place again. I felt numb. I had no emotion and I was incapable of feeling anything but pity for myself. My body was there, but my mind was not. I felt as if I were in another dimension.

I finally decided that I could no longer tolerate being there with everyone. I hated myself, and I couldn't bear to have anyone else see this in me. I knew that it was best for me leave. I told Frank to stay and enjoy himself but that I was leaving to go home. All I wanted was to be in my bed. My bed was the only place where I found some comfort, because I didn't need to face anyone or anything. In my bed, I didn't have to face the world! That was where I needed to be.

On my drive home, I came to the conclusion that I didn't want to live anymore, at least not like this. Although I had no plan to take my life, I was numb to the thought of suicide. It did not scare me anymore and that was unsettling to me.

I knew that Frank, my kids, parents, sister and brother, and good friends would be hurt by this act. But that didn't matter so much to me. What mattered to me most was that I would not be hurting anymore. Depression is a very selfish illness and has NO mercy for anyone. My rationale was that they would be okay eventually, and they wouldn't need to be part of my ordeal anymore. Looking back now on that moment, it is very scary to realize that I was at peace with the thought of ending my life. I had never been at peace with this idea before.

By the time I reached my driveway, my eyes were welled up with tears. I put my car into parking gear, removed the key, and got out. I walked briskly to the front door, and the tears had now begun to roll down my cheeks. I struggled to unlock the door. Once inside the house, I slammed the door closed and ran up to my bedroom. I never made it to my bed because I fell to my knees. I began screaming and crying to God. I was angry with Him!! With my head looking up to the ceiling of my bedroom, I yelled, "I need Your help! My family needs Your help! Where are You???? Lord, where are YOU!? Why are You putting me through this again?" Now my fists were banging on the floor and my head was down. Tears were now streaming down my face. I could taste the salt of my tears as they flowed over my lips and around the corners of my mouth. "God, I do not want to **live** anymore! Is this what You wanted me to say? I hate what I am doing to my family. The guilt that I feel is unbearable! They do not deserve this roller coaster ride! How much more can they take? How much more can I take? Please Lord, help me! I beg You Lord, please help me!" The screaming pleas were loud and my voice was beginning to crack.

I remained on my knees and closed my eyes. And in my mind's eye, I could see and feel God standing on my right side. But I could also see and feel the presence of dark and evil energy on my left. The evil presence on my left was trying to "console" me and ultimately take over my soul. I felt as if this energy wanted to remove the pain for me. I could feel myself moving towards him because he was going to make me feel better. The evil was fighting with God to claim my soul, and maybe I should give in to him. I was feeling numb and hopeless, and the thought of taking my life was becoming real. I began to think that this was how it was supposed to end for me. In this moment, I felt in my heart that everyone's life would be better if I were not part of it anymore. Why would I want to live like this anyway? The anger, depression, guilt and loneliness had finally won. My spirit had been broken and my faith was gone. My soul was going to belong to the evil entity that I could feel and see to my left.

Just then, as if to catch him by accident, I could see the face of evil look up at God with a smirk and laugh. It was as if he were telling God that he had won the prize of my soul, and how dumb of me to fall for his tricks. I felt no love or caring from this energy anymore! All I could feel or see was pain and suffering. Before I would let him take me, I managed to scream, "Oh God I need You now. Please save me!!"

At that point, I felt enraged. My eyes opened wide. I spoke directly to the evil presence. "How dare you play with my life as if it is a game! You are playing with not only my life but the lives of my children and my family." I became so angry and defensive. I was trying to protect my soul like a parent protects his or her child. I knew that this was God's help that I was receiving to fight off the evil. God had given me the strength to wipe away the tears from my cheeks and fight.

I turned to look at the bed where I had spent so many days and nights. It was my private tomb. I had spent hours staring at a blank television screen and hours crying to the point of exhaustion. I hated that bed, but I knew that I would return to it immediately and without question, if that was what God had planned for me. If I was going to leave this life, it would not be by my own hand! I would not allow myself to bring the debilitating pain that I had been suffering for fifteen years to the people who loved me. I would not give this evil energy the satisfaction of distorting my children by having me take my own life. I crawled back into bed with a renewed light and with the decision to stay and fight.

That night, I ventured down the path to recovery for the final time. Days grew into weeks and weeks grew into months. I continued with my therapy and medication again, and I started to return to normal. When I became well again, I took time to do research. I was looking for answers. I wanted to find out why my life had led me down the road of depression and anxiety, and what lesson that I was supposed to learn from it. I pored over many books on empowerment, life after death and Heaven, all for a better understanding. This is when the next part of my amazing and magical journey began.

PART TWO
MY BLESSING

CHAPTER 8
DELIVERING HEAVEN'S MESSAGE

In April of 2013, I was invited to see a medium/ psychic with a couple of my friends. I walked into her office and saw a tall blond woman wearing a lot of jewelry and make up. I wasn't sure about this reading that I was about to have, but I was curious and excited to hear what she had to say. I wasn't a true believer in this, but I was open minded. Her name was Olivia, and she asked me to take a seat. I sat in the closest chair. She then asked me if I had any questions or if I wanted to speak to anyone in spirit. I wasn't very prepared for this reading and had no agenda. She then asked if I had a photo of my family, so I quickly rummaged through my purse to find one, and I handed it to her. I have been to other psychics before, for fun, and I didn't find any of them to be very accurate. What Olivia was able to tell me was so different from anything that I had ever heard from a psychic before. She was able to tell me about my husband and children. She described their personalities perfectly. She could tell me where they were last week and give me a good idea of what their futures may look like. She spoke to my grandparents and to Frank's grandmother by using psychometry. This is a technique used to make a psychic connection to a spirit by holding a personal object that belonged to the deceased person. Olivia gave me messages from the grandparents. I was able to validate these messages. It was really cool, but what she told me about myself left me stunned.

Olivia told me that if I did not get to know God better, I would find myself crawled up in a ball, depressed, lonely, and looking for help again. My mouth dropped open. It was like a spike was driven into my heart. This had been my biggest fear for so long, and these words came from out of nowhere. It shook me to my core. She continued to tell me that I am psychic and that I am an "empath". I asked her to spell it, because I had never heard that term before. I was told that I had a connection to God that needed to be uncovered, and that I was on a journey of self-discovery.

I began researching books on psychics and on empaths. The more I read, the more I began to understand myself.

The pieces to the puzzle (my life) were all coming together. The definition of an empath is a person who is highly sensitive to the emotions and energy around them. This extreme sensitivity to other people's energy applies to family members, as well as strangers. An empath is like an emotional sponge with the ability to absorb the emotions of others without knowing it. When an empath absorbs too much negative emotion it can trigger panic attacks and depression. That was it! That was me! "I can't believe this is a thing", I thought to myself. It was a relief to think that this was the answer, but I wasn't totally convinced. It took months of reading and research on empaths to convince me that this was an ability that I actually had.

Now that I understood that I was an empath, what was I to do about it? Why would God give this empathic ability to someone, if it were not for some good reason? I would pray and ask God what I should do with this. I didn't want to feel the emotions of other people. Why do I need to feel this way, and what good did it do anyone, for me to feel their emotions? It felt more like a curse, to have this ability.

I was encouraged by my friend Dawn to explore this and to read about grounding and protection. Dawn had helped me through my latest deep depression and was convinced that I was an Empath. We grabbed every book on psychic development and protection. We learned to put a white light of protection around us as a shield, to stop the absorption of negative energy from other people. I was desperate to learn how to stop the waves of unexpected panic and sadness that would at times affect me so strongly.

CHAPTER 9
MEETING JAN

Five months later, in August 2013, a friend whom I had known for more than thirty years invited me to attend a meditation class. Other than hearing about meditation and seeing people doing it on television, I was unfamiliar with the idea. But something about attending this class excited me. My friend, Lily, and I made a plan to attend on the following Monday night. I really began to look forward to attending this class. The whole idea was intriguing, even though I still didn't know what to expect.

Unfortunately, when Monday rolled around, Lily was unable to go. I was very disappointed. But I had a nagging feeling inside of me that urged me to attend the class on my own. I was not the adventurous type. I would never do something like this on my own. But the urge to go won out over my feeling of uneasiness. I put the address into my GPS and off to the small New Jersey town I went.

This was so out of character for me. I never even told my family where I was going. I didn't even leave an address so that they would know where to look for me if I failed to return home. I was having a difficult time finding the place. I had no idea what type of building I was looking for. I didn't know if it was an office building, or a store, or a house. I drove up and down the same street at least three or four times. I was about to go home when I decided to pull over. I started talking to God. "God, okay this is it. If I don't see this place, then it is not meant for me to be here." With that being said, I looked to my right and saw a small sign on an old eerie looking Victorian style house. The sign said "Spirituality of N. J." I could not believe what I was seeing. I stumbled upon what I was looking for. It was meant for me to find this place.

At this point, I laughed to myself, and thought that there was no way that I was going to go into this place alone. But then my inner voice told me that it was okay to go in. This was the same voice that led me to the spot in the first place. So again, I listened to this voice and got out of the car. I looked at my surroundings and noticed a church and a small cemetery across the street. "A little creepy", I thought to myself. I approached the house and knocked on the door. There was no answer. My logical self told me to just turn around, get back into the car, and go home. This was my chance to turn away. But once again, I listened to my inner voice, and continued to move forward, and entered the building.

I opened up the old creaky door to a set of steps. As I began to climb, I could sense the age of this building by the old musty smell. It was dark and dreary. The steps were creaking and very steep. I grabbed onto the ball at the top of the baluster as I began to climb, and the ball came off in my hand. I struggled to put it back in place, before anyone saw me. As I continued up the steps into a dark hallway, my heart was pounding. I thought to myself that I may die here or meet the devil himself!

The feeling of fight or flight came over me and I felt my face begin to flush. I decided that I needed to go. This was not safe. I turned around to leave, and at that very moment, a woman opened the door behind me. She had a very pleasant face and a welcoming smile. "Hello," she said. "Are you here for the class?" There was no turning back now. I would need to jump over her in order to get to the door. The steps were so narrow, that I couldn't maneuver around her. With hesitancy in my voice, I said, "Yes." I turned and continued up the stairs to the room where the class was to be held.

I laugh to myself now, when I think about that night. I did not know then, that this was a new chapter in my journey. I did not know then, how that night would change so much about me. I did not know then, that the voice that I kept hearing was called INTUITION.

CHAPTER 10

FIRST SPIRIT VISITATION

Grandmom Mary

I started to attend Jan's classes every week. I found the classes very informative and relaxing. I learned how to protect my energy and how to limit taking on other people energy (their "stuff"). My first connection with spirits in Jan's meditation class was about to take place.

I had calmed my mind as I listened to Jan channel her meditation, and I was visualizing a beautiful white cloud at the top of my head. The white cloud was rotating, and started slowly descending down onto my body, as per Jan's channeled message from spirit. It didn't take me long to lose track of Jan's meditation. I found myself standing before three of my grandparents and one of my husband's grandmothers, all of whom had previously passed over. My grandparents were excited and happy, but also surprised to see me.

The only one who wasn't surprised to see me was Frank's grandmother, Mary. She had been expecting me. She was so excited that she was jumping up and down. In life, Mary was a sweet woman and I was very fond of her. My husband and I started dating when we were sixteen, so Grand mom Mary was like another grandmother to me.

During my reading with Olivia about four months earlier, she told me that Grandmom Mary wanted me to write a letter to her, and then she wanted me to bury it outside my house. But she didn't want me to tell anyone else. I was also told that she would get in touch with me somehow. I was leery about the whole thing, but I did it, thinking that it wouldn't hurt anyone. I buried the letter outside of my house, in the flower bed.

Two days after I buried the letter, we were preparing for Avery's prom. It was a beautiful May evening, and the family came to see Avery off for her big event. After everyone left, I was sitting in my office, and Frank came in from outside holding a pair of black rosary beads. We thought that they belonged to my son, but it would have been extremely out of character for him to have rosaries outside of the house. I asked Frank where he found them, and he said that they were in the flower bed. Puzzled, I walked out of my office to look at the rosary beads. They were weathered but in good shape. Frank showed me where he found them and they were in the spot where I had placed the letter. I was shocked, because I knew that they were not there earlier. I called every person who had been at my house that evening, to ask if they had lost the rosary beads. I also questioned my son. No one knew anything about the rosary beads. I knew in my heart that they came from Grandmom Mary. She was letting me know that she is around me and my home.

That is why she was not surprised to see me that night, in my meditation class. She was excited to tell the rest of the grandparents that she knew that I would do what she had asked of me, and that I would come to see them.

CHAPTER 11
A Message for Dominic

I met a lot of new people in Jan's class, and one man stood out from the rest. His name was Dominic, and he was a typical Italian older man whom you might meet in the city where I grew up. Dominic came to class with his black hair slicked back, gold chains around his neck, and satin jogging suit. He was a very nice man, but not the typical person I would have expected to meet there. In my mind, I expected to meet people who seemed to be more spiritual, earthy, and maybe even a little "hippy-like". I enjoyed hearing his story and found him interesting. Everyone in this class was interesting. It was a bunch of people meditating, and discussing spirituality, spirits and spirit visitation, and I felt right at home.

I enjoyed meditation, and I even started to meditate in the morning, in my bedroom, where I kept my books, CD player, and candles. I put together a little "zen den" for myself, and on occasion, Avery would join me. One morning, before work, I sat in my bedroom with my legs crossed, listening to my meditation CD. I started to drift into a calm, peaceful trance, and soon I was in a place of total calm. When I could not hear the voices and the instructions from my CD, a vision of Dominic appeared in my mind's eye. He was sitting in a chair, and the chair moved from my left to my right and then started to fade out of my view, to my right. Coming in from my left side was a very deep voice of a man of Italian decent. "Tell him he needs to take care of himself. He needs to go to the gym" is what this voice said. The next thing I heard was the words "excessive drinking and smoking". My eyes popped open and I was confused with what had just happened. Did I just make contact with spirit? For the rest of the day, I had a nagging feeling that I needed to get in touch with Dominic. But if I did, what would I say? "I think that your dead relative has a message for you"? He may think that I was a nut! However, I thought to myself that he must be open to this stuff if he attends meditation classes. My next thought was, "Well, if I want to know whether I had made contact with spirit, I need to talk to him, and he may be more understanding than anyone else".

I was scheduled for a class on the next evening, and I thought, "Perfect, I will tell him then". I got to class the next evening, and Dominic never showed up. Ugh! I asked Jan if she had his number, but no go! I thought to myself that it wasn't meant to be, and that I may have just saved myself from some embarrassment.

The next morning, I started the meditation as I did the day before. I put my CD on and got comfortable. Then I closed my eyes. "YOU DIDN'T TELL HIM"?, was what I heard. I knew that it was the man from the day before, and somehow, I knew that it was Dominic's grandfather. I responded back in my mind "I tried, but he wasn't there". Then I heard "You need to tell him. You need to try harder". That day, I was determined to reach Dominic. "After all, I don't need a dead man scolding me again", I thought jokingly. That morning, in my office, I began searching for him on a website that introduced people to local meeting groups for like-minded people, like wine groups, movie groups etc. I found Dominic on that site and sent him a private message. I said, "Hi Dominic, this is Victoria from class, and I think that I may have a message for you, from someone who has crossed over. It may not be for you at all but I would like to talk to you", and then left him my number.

I left it open-ended so that I wouldn't look ridiculous if I was wrong!

I hadn't heard from him all day, but as I was cleaning up my desk and getting ready to leave for the night, my phone rang. It was Dominic. "Hi Victoria, you have a message for me?" I began to tell him about my experience during meditation. I told him about the man who wanted me to contact him. Dominic spoke up right away and said, "Yes, yes, that's my grandfather and you are the third person who told me that he was trying to contact me". He continued to tell me about his health problem, and his habits of drinking and smoking. I only heard half of what he was saying, because I was in shock. Isabel was still at work with me, and I could see her in the next office. Isabel was very interested in this stuff, and was eager to know what would happen when he called back.

I waved Isabel over to my office and mouthed to her that it was his grandfather. Isabel's mouth fell open, and she chuckled and smiled. My next thought was that I am just a good guesser. Even though I am having these experiences, I am not sure that I believe it myself! But this is cool and I was hooked, I wanted to learn more......

CHAPTER 12
WHAT WILL MY FAMILY THINK?

At home, during my morning meditations, I quickly started making contact with other spirits. I would receive messages from my aunts and uncles who had crossed over. I would call my cousins to relay these messages to them. You can imagine their surprise, to hear that I had been talking to their parents who had passed over, and that I have received a message for them. I knew that it would be shocking and somewhat unsettling, for them to learn that I had this ability, which seemed to manifest itself out of thin air. It was difficult for me also, to believe that I was communicating with spirits. I felt uneasy about sharing this with them. I thought, "What if I am wrong about the information that I am about to deliver to them? What if the information that I am giving to them made NO sense to them? How would I explain myself to them, and how can I apologize for upsetting them?" It would be easier to just ignore these messages, and go on with my day as though nothing had happened. But I couldn't do that.

I would often hear in my mind that I need to tell them, and that I needed to trust in God, and that I was chosen to do this work. I did find it fascinating and I was very curious to see whether the messages would mean anything to anyone. My curiosity always won out and I would place the call. To my surprise, the messages always meant something, and my cousins knew exactly what their mother or father was talking about. It always felt great to make them happy and to help them heal, but most of all, to help them believe that there is more to life than this physical place on earth. I quickly wanted to make contact again, and as soon as I did, the doubt would set in. Maybe I was wrong, and did I really know what I was doing? It took courage for me to contact the living as a service for the dead. Now I had begun contacting friends, co-workers, and strangers, with messages from their loved ones in spirit. It was as though the word went out to the spirit world that I had this ability, and that I was open for business! I would receive messages from spirits while in the shower, while driving to work, while waiting in doctors' offices, and while sitting in restaurants. I thought there must be some way to control this. I could see how this would test anyone's sense of reality.

I knew that I needed to learn more about contacting the spirit world and relaying messages. So I started to take development classes with Teresa, a wonderful teacher. I was very lucky to be living in an area of the country where believers operated numerous development circles. I needed to learn all that I could, in order to get answers to my many questions. I knew that if I intended to continue to give messages, I needed to learn how to give accurate, validating, information as well. I was fortunate to have found three wonderful teachers, in Jan, Teresa and Stacey. I am very grateful for their love and encouragement. I believe that God puts our teachers in places where we can find them all along our journey.

CHAPTER 13
AND THE BEAT GOES ON

Spirits now make contact with me almost daily. I will relate just a few stories here, because my experiences seem to be endless.

Jim

I was traveling with my extended family on a group vacation, and we were stuck in an airport because our flight had been delayed. My niece and her new husband Jim had joined our trip, and he had asked me for a reading while we were delayed at the airport. Jim was skeptical that anyone could have the ability to communicate with spirits, but he was very curious. I was not real comfortable with his request because of his skepticism, and because we were in an airport.

I didn't know if I could make a connection with spirit, if there were so many people around. If I was unsuccessful, that would be proof to him that communicating with spirit is nonsense.

Jim and I moved to a more private waiting area in the airport. I asked him to pray with me, and to silently ask the friend or family member with whom he wanted to communicate, to come to us. We bowed our heads and I said a quiet prayer. I prayed for guidance and for only positive messages for Jim's well being. I then lifted my head and in my mind's eye, I saw an older man near a lake or a river? I asked Jim if he had lost a grandfather, and with skepticism in his voice, he told me that he had. The next thing that I sensed was that his grandfather had taught Jim to fish, and that his name was John. Jim, at this point, was shocked, but still not convinced. I proceeded by telling Jim that his grandfather was proud of him and that he wanted to make sure that Jim knew this. He also approved of the relationship between Jim and my niece. This was very moving for Jim, because that was a question that he wanted to ask his grandfather.

"I sense a dog around him," I told Jim. I was not looking straight at Jim, because I didn't want to lose my concentration. I wanted to give him the best possible reading. Jim broke down into tears with his face in his hands. I knew that the reading needed to end. After Jim composed himself, he shared with me that he didn't expect anyone to come through. But in the beginning of the reading, when I told him to ask for someone who he wanted to come through, he did in fact ask for his grandfather. He asked his grandfather if he was proud of him and the decisions that he had made in his life. The last thing that he had asked his grandfather during his prayer before we began the reading was, "if this is real, can you please bring the family dog with you?" When I told him that I sensed a dog with his grandfather, Jim had the confirmation that he needed. He knew that his grandfather had come through. He is now a believer.

Claire

I was just starting my journey into mediumship. After I had taken several classes, I decided that it would be best for me to start practicing by giving readings to people. My sister had a friend, Claire. They had been friends for quite a while. They were co-workers. I had been introduced to her at one time, but I did not know her well at all. I knew nothing of her past or of her family and she agreed have a reading with me.

At this time, seeing spirits was starting to become a routine for me, as I would frequently see them appear in my thoughts and dreams. At times, I even saw them standing at my bedside. They always had messages for me to give to their loved ones and friends. So, it was not a surprise to me, when a few nights before I was to meet with Claire at my sister's house, I had a vision. I had gotten into bed and closed my eyes. In a flash, I saw Claire's face and an older man. I assumed that this was Claire's dad. He was wearing a mechanic's uniform. I heard very distinctly the words "stroke" and "tattoo on forearm." The next day I called my sister. She had spoken to Claire, and Claire had confirmed that what I had heard was meaningful.

On the night of Claire's reading, I was expecting her dad to come through. But to my surprise, her brother came through instead. When her brother came through, he was shining and happy. He was showing me things that he liked to do when he was here on earth. He let me see him playing basketball and working in his garage. He also led me into the woods. I could see his boots walking, and crushing the leaves and twigs. I could smell the aroma of the forest and feel the temperature on my skin. This was the area where he had been shot. He brought me there for his sister's validation, so that there would be no doubt about the messages that he needed to share with her. He did not want her to dwell on the circumstances of this event, or of his death. He knew that her heart was still broken and unsettled. He wanted her to remember the good times that they shared in life. He wanted her to let go of the past, and to move forward and continue to be happy. He wanted her to understand that he is in heaven and is in peace, and that the rest is unimportant.

Just before the reading ended, her father returned. After my original contact with her dad, Claire had asked for validation from him. Before she met with me, she asked him to confirm the image of his tattoo, and to show it to me. Her father did just that. Claire shared with me that before our reading began, she also prayed for her brother. I always have my clients say a prayer when we begin, so that they can ask their loved ones to come through to us.

Claire often thanks me for the closure that she received from that reading. I was very happy that I could give her the healing that she needed from her loved ones.

Stacey

Dr. Stacey Maxwell was my instructor and mentor for my Mind, Body, Spirit Practitioner course. I completed her amazing course in record time. It was fun, interesting and motivating. During the process of taking her course, Dr. Stacey and I spoke over the phone and online many times, and we built a very nice friendship. One afternoon, Dr. Stacey asked if I would be willing to give her a reading over the phone. I had done this before with childhood friends and family. This time, I knew that the pressure would be on me to perform. I was nervous, but we set a date and time for us to connect.

Before I called her for the reading, I got comfortable in my spare bedroom. I lit some candles and I prepared the room. I said a prayer to my spirit guides, and asked them for guidance. In my prayers, I told my guides how important this reading was for me, and that I really needed their help. When I got Dr. Stacey on the phone, I asked her to say a silent prayer, asking her family members and friends to come through to us.

My spirit guides came through for me, in a big way. Dr. Stacey heard from five spirits. Some came at her request and some on their own accord. The first spirit to come was an old client of Dr. Stacey's. He wanted to thank her for her help during his time on earth. The second spirit was her great grandmother whom she had never met. She came through in a loving and caring manner, and talked a little about the family history. The next was one of her grandmothers, who came through asking for forgiveness and understanding. She had validated herself with familiar clothing and posture and habits.

The next two spirits were also her grandparents, and they came through wearing familiar clothing, as well. Her grandmother spoke of a necklace that had a meaning of validation for Dr. Stacey. It wasn't an immediate memory for Stacey, but she did remember it, and was surprised that she had forgotten it. Her grandfather showed me a very clear picture of a watch in details that I could not know about. He reminded her about the conversations that they had prior to his death. They had been joking about how his watch had stopped working, and was not keeping time. Grandpa told her that this was God's way of saying that his time on earth was over. He crossed over a few days after the watch stopped working. He was at peace. This experience brought Stacey great comfort, and hearing the stories that she had almost forgotten brought priceless new memory.

CHAPTER 14

MY CHURCH

I had a major concern about how my new found abilities might conflict with my Roman Catholic faith. Frank and I were both born and raised in the Catholic Church and attended Catholic schools. Both sets of parents were and are devout Catholics, and I wasn't sure how all of this would sit with them. Of course, I knew that they loved me and believed in me, but did they understand and approve of it? The one person whom I was the most concerned about was my Dad. He was always very faithful to his religion, and directly involved with the IHN ministry in particular.

He found all of this so interesting and fascinating, as I did, but the position of the Church on this subject was concerning to him as well as to me. I wanted to make an appointment with Fr. Sam, one of the priests in my parish, but I was concerned about the way he might accept my revelation. I had read stories about other mediums who spoke to their pastors about their abilities, and they were shamed and dismissed, as if they were doing something evil.

I knew that what I was doing was not wrong, and that this was something which needed to be embraced as a form of healing, and as a confirmation that Heaven does exist.

To my pleasant surprise, the reaction that I received from Fr. Sam was one of understanding and belief. I was told that the Church acknowledges people with this gift. It is my understanding that the Church doesn't so much disapprove of this practice, but has grave concerns with the integrity of the practitioners, and with the safety of the manner in which the messages are delivered. In this healing practice, safety is paramount, and education is really required. This cannot be entered into lightly, because it comes with great responsibility.

My Dad spoke to a priest who had come to visit my mother while she had a short stay in the hospital. My father asked the priest if he believed that God would allow people to have the ability to speak to spirits of the deceased. The look that the priest gave my father said it all. "And Why

Not?!?", he responded. He went on to explain that, as long as the experience was not scaring me, or making me upset, it would probably be fine. However, he warned that I needed to be very careful, because there are evil spirits lurking, and care must be taken in order to keep them out.

Another priest told my Dad that his own father had come and visited him shortly after crossing over, and told him that Saint Anthony had come to help him to make the transition from this life to the next. "Heaven is for real", he said.

Now, with these concerns in check, I feel free to pursue my practice without the reservations that were haunting me. I am just that much further convinced that God is guiding my actions.

AFTERWORD

My journey is far from complete, but as I look back and assess my past, I think about my depression. We certainly need doctors, and we need the medications. Without these, I may not have made it this far. In my case, and in the case of others, of whom I am now aware, there can be additional issues at play, of which many well educated doctors have little or no knowledge.

For years, I was feeling the emotions of others, and believing that they were mine. But God allowed me to discover gifts which are never discussed in normal conversation. Most people refuse to believe that these gifts exist. I know that they come from God, and that He wants me to use them to help His people. We are all one in His Love.

So, far, I have discovered that I have been given several abilities, such as:

- Mediumship (the ability to communicate with individuals who have passed over to the spirit world),
- Clairaudience (the ability to hear words and sounds from the spirit world),
- Claircognizance (the ability to physically know something without being told),
- Clairgustance (the ability to perceive tastes without actually tasting anything),
- Clairsentience (the ability to sense or feel the presence of those from the spirit world),
- Clairvoyance (the ability to see spirits from the other side, through the mind's eye)

I hope to be able to continue to use these gifts to further the Glory of God.

AFTERWARD

Victoria and I have been best friends since we were 15 years old. I was the new girl in the 10th grade and had a rough time making friends and adjusting to my new environment. In January of my sophomore year, Victoria befriended me in Health class. From the moment we talked, our personalities clicked and 33 years later, we are still in each other's lives, not only as best friends, but we are also family because we are married to brothers.

Victoria and I have been together through the happiest moments of our lives and the lowest moments of our lives. We've cheered each other on and we've picked each other up. The uniqueness of our relationship is that we are honest with each other. I can truly say that in all of these years, we've never had a fight. She knows me inside and out and I know her inside and out.

Most of what you have read in this book, I have experienced with Victoria. I felt her pain and cried when she suffered her depressions. I remember specifically crying when she experienced her first depression because I didn't understand what happened to my friend who was happy-go-lucky and bubbly. The friend who had a solution for all of my problems couldn't find a solution to her own. That was heartbreaking to me.

When Victoria decided that she would write this book, she asked me if I knew anyone who could help her. I quickly volunteered for two reasons. First, it has always been a dream of mine to write a book. Second, who better to write a book about her than me who had first-hand knowledge of her experiences and could help her put her thoughts on paper. Working on this book together, has just been another wonderful chapter in our friendship.

To watch Victoria emerge throughout her spiritual journey has been inspiring to me. I am so proud of the way she has pulled herself up so many times and has gotten to this point in her life. She has taught me so much about spirituality and has helped me on my own personal life journey.

Victoria, God bless you my friend...XOXO

Much love and success,

Kasey

Printed in the United States
By Bookmasters